W9-COF-770

I'm Sorry We Quarrelled

I'm Sorry We Quarrelled

with photographs by
Hy Fujita

Edited
by Victor Allen

STANYAN BOOKS   RANDOM HOUSE

To Charles Hale Matthews

Come now, and let us reason together.

— Isaiah   1:18

We like a man to come right out and say
what he thinks — if we agree with him.

— Mark Twain

✹ ✹ ✹

A long argument means that both
parties are wrong.   — Voltaire

✹ ✹ ✹

Quarrels would never last long if the fault
was only on one side.

— Duc de la Rochefoucauld

To err is human; to forgive, divine.

— **Alexander Pope**

Life appears to me too short to be spent in nursing animosity or registering wrong.

— **Charlotte Brontë**

I dislike arguments of any kind.
They are always vulgar, and often convincing.

— **Oscar Wilde**

※ ※ ※

Opposition inflames the enthusiast,
never converts him.

— **Johann von Schiller**

※ ※ ※

Though I can't make her love me, there is
great satisfaction in quarreling with her.

— **Richard Sheridan**

In a false quarrel there is no true valour.

— **William Shakespeare**

Weakness on both sides, is, as we know, the trait of all quarrels.

– **Voltaire**

I never take my own side in a quarrel.

– **Robert Frost**

There is no good in arguing with the inevitable. The only argument available with an east wind is to put on your overcoat.

– **James Russell Lowell**

Hearts are like flowers; they remain open
to the softly falling dew, but shut up in the
violent downpour of rain.

— **Jean Paul Richter**

Forgiveness swells the tide of love.

— **Michel de Montaigne**

Never let the sun set on a quarrel.

— **Dr. Louisa Duffe Booth**

The quarrel is a very pretty quarrel as it stands; we should only spoil it by trying to explain it.

— Richard Sheridan

God turns his back on those who quarrel
among themselves.

— **Mahatma Gandhi**

❀ ❀ ❀

The evils of controversy are transitory;
while its benefits are permanent.

— **Robert Hall**

The worst kind of quarrels are with oneself.

— Henry David Thoreau

Quarreling makes the heart grow fonder.

— **Catherine Frey**

※ ※ ※

Other people's quarrels always seem petty
until you have reason to fight about the
very same thing yourself.

— **William Hazlitt**

Fight with me — for what are friends for?

— **Will Rogers**

Once a woman has forgiven her man,
she must not reheat his sins for breakfast.

— **Marlene Dietrich**

He that studies revenge keeps his own wounds
green when they otherwise would heal
and do well.

— **Francis Bacon**

🌾 🌾 🌾

I don't care any more if you were right.
I only care . . .

— **Jensey Cooper**

🌾 🌾 🌾

I didn't believe you until your heart
got out of hand and in the way.

— **Sister Clarice Kopell**

Few quarrels are as serious when they're
over as they were when started.

— **Voltaire**

✻ ✻ ✻

I'll remember what you said if you go away.
I'll forget if you'd stay.

— **Walter Harvey**

✻ ✻ ✻

I'm in love, I'm not listening — try again.

— **Oscar Wilde**

Feel honored — I've never quarreled
with anybody I didn't like.

— **Randa Lee**

※ ※ ※

An argument is the only game where the
winner is sometimes the loser.

— **Thomas Jefferson**

※ ※ ※

To be wronged is nothing unless you
continue to remember it.

— **Confucius**

If I listen I have the advantage;
if I speak, others have it.

— **Arabic proverb**

🌾 🌾 🌾

Only dogs should quarrel — they are more
forgiving than people.

— **Fred Allen**

🌾 🌾 🌾

Our argument is like an instrumental —
the words don't make sense.

— **Bevins Jay**

Even the most sincere apology can't take all the sting out of a quarrel — only love can.

— **Bessie Lorraine Boles**

❧ ❧ ❧

We pardon as long as we love

— **Duc de la Rochefoucauld**

❧ ❧ ❧

A man's opinions are of much more value than his arguments.

— **Oliver Wendell Holmes**

Least said — soonest mended.

                              — Miguel de Cervantes

They say never go to bed and leave a quarrel unsettled, but what if you're quarrelling about going to bed?

— **Alexandre Drey**

No one can be in perfect accord with any one but himself.

— **Arthur Schopenhauer**

❀ ❀ ❀

When anger arises, think of the consequences.

— **Confucius**

❀ ❀ ❀

The only conquests which are permanent, and leave no regrets are our conquests over ourselves.

— **Napoleon I**

❀ ❀ ❀

Forget injuries, never forget kindnesses.

— **Chinese proverb**

❀ ❀ ❀

Next to knowing when to seize an opportunity, the most important thing in life is to know when to forego an advantage.

— **Benjamin Disraeli**

And throughout all eternity,
I forgive you, you forgive me. — **William Blake**

🌾 🌾 🌾

"I can forgive but I cannot forget"
is only another way of saying,
"I cannot forgive."

— **Henry Ward Beecher**

🌾 🌾 🌾

Is it not better to forget than to remember
and regret?

— **Letitia Landon**

🌾 🌾 🌾

Better by far that you should forget and smile
than that you should remember and be sad.

— **Christina Georgina Rossetti**

Forgiveness ought to be like a cancelled note —
torn in half and burned up; so that it can
never be shown against the man.

— **Henry Ward Beecher**

In quarreling truth is always lost.

— Publilius Syrus

❋ ❋ ❋

Revenge is the poor delight of little minds.

— Decimus Juvenal

❋ ❋ ❋

An argument needs not reason,
nor a friendship. **— Ibycus**

Two wrongs don't make a right.
Two rights can make a wrong.
— 19th C. proverb

Be calm in arguing; for fierceness makes
error a fault and truth discourtesy.

— **George Herbert**

❦ ❦ ❦

The test of a man or woman's breeding
is how they behave in a quarrel.

— **George Bernard Shaw**

❦ ❦ ❦

When the candles are out,
our arguments will be over.   — **Epictetus**

❦ ❦ ❦

Happy, thrice happy and more, are they
whom an unknown bond united and
whose love shall know no sundering quarrels
so long as they shall live.

— **Horace**

If we open a quarrel between the past and the present, we shall find that we have lost the future.

—Winston Churchill

I would not forgive you could I but forget you.

— **François Rabelais**

☙ ☙ ☙

Apologies must look to the past with repentance and to the future with watchfulness.

— **Oliver Goldsmith**

☙ ☙ ☙

We never ask God to forgive anybody except where we haven't.

— **Elbert Hubbard**

Our reconciliation is like ice —
but let it be ice melted, not ice broken.

—**Thomas Carlyle**

☘ ☘ ☘

Disagreement is the first step
on the path of discovery.

— **Henry Fielding**

To do so no more is the truest repentance.

— **Martin Luther**

❉ ❉ ❉

To regret deeply is to live afresh.

— **Henry David Thoreau**

❉ ❉ ❉

The heart that is soonest awake to the flowers
is always the first to be touched by the thorns.

—**Thomas Moore**

❉ ❉ ❉

The dew of compassion is a tear.

— **Lord Byron**

❉ ❉ ❉

If you wish to please people, you begin by
understanding them.

— **Charles Reade**

It is never worthwhile to suggest doubts
in order to show how cleverly
we can answer them.

— **Richard Whately**

🌾 🌾 🌾

He who knows only his own side of the case,
knows little of that.

— **John Stuart Mills**

🌾 🌾 🌾

Unfortunately, forgiveness for those we know
is rarer than pity for those we do not know.

— **George Eliot**

🌾 🌾 🌾

An ounce of apology is worth a
pound of loneliness.

— **Joseph Joubert**

Better are the blows of a friend
than the false kisses of an enemy.

— **Thomas à Becket**

❀ ❀ ❀

An obstinate man does not hold opinions —
they hold him.

— **Abraham Lincoln**

❀ ❀ ❀

Sometimes the best gain is to lose.

— **George Herbert**

❀ ❀ ❀

No persons are more frequently wrong
than those who will not admit they are wrong.

— **Duc de la Rochefoucauld**

Nature has given us two ears, two eyes,
and but one tongue — to the end that we
should hear and see more than we speak.

— **Socrates**

✻ ✻ ✻

Anyone may quarrel — only fools
continue at it.   — **Cicero**

✻ ✻ ✻

Teach me to feel another's woe,
To hide the fault I see,
Forgiveness I to others show
That forgiveness show to me.

— **Alexander Pope**

If you want enemies, excel others;
if friends, let others excel you.

— **Charles Colton**

Give me your love —
I have enough arguments of my own.

— **Johann Wolfgang von Goethe**

No person can seek to be perfect
without starting quarrels with everyone else.
In imperfection there is love.

— **Blaise Pascal**

I see my image in your eyes dissolved
in disappointed tears. — **Rod McKuen**

We argued. But then I saw your face
and knew I had lost — not by being wrong,
but by being right.

— **Anatole France**

☙ ☙ ☙

The head argues; the heart forgives.

— **Jean Jacques Rousseau**

☙ ☙ ☙

I am right and you are wrong.
But why do I miss you so?

—**William Cooper**

Lovers' quarrels are the renewal of love.

— **Terence**

If you cry as the result of my argument,
I have lost more than words.

— **Lao-tse**

🌾 🌾 🌾

The quarrels of lovers are like summer
storms — everything is more beautiful
when they've passed.

— **Suzanne Necker**

🌾 🌾 🌾

How many times have we walked on this trail,
argued about this question, separated with
this anger . . . And still tomorrow —
we will love.

— **Lord Byron**